THE ONE MINUTE COACH

THE ONE MINUTE COACH

Change your life one minute at a time!

Masha Malka

Published by
Hybrid Global Publishing
301 E 57th Street, 4th fl
New York, NY 10022

Copyright © 2018 by Masha Malka

All rights reserved. No part of this book may be reproduced or transmitted in any form or by in any means, electronic or mechanical, including photocopying, recording, or by any information storage and retrieval system, without the written permission of the Publisher, except where permitted by law.

Manufactured in the United States of America, or in the
United Kingdom when distributed elsewhere.

Malka, Masha
The One Minute Coach: Change Your Life One Minute at a Time!
ISBN: 978-1-938015-98-4
eBook: 978-1-938015-99-1

Cover design: Anna Polonsky
Interior design: Medlar Publishing Solutions Pvt Ltd., India
Editing: Cary Johnston
Artwork: Anna Polonsky

www.mashamalka.com

TABLE OF CONTENTS

Forward by Cary Johnston   viii
Introduction From the Author   xi

Part 1: Freedom to Be Who You Are

Chapter 1	Whose Life Are You Living?	2
Chapter 2	The 'Impossible' is Often the Untried	4
Chapter 3	If they Can Do It, So Can You!	6
Chapter 4	Are You Starving Your Soul?	8
Chapter 5	What Fulfills You?	10
Chapter 6	Freedom to Be Who You Are	12
Chapter 7	It All Comes Down to Faith	14

Part 2: The Secrets of People Who Are Successful

Chapter 8	The Secrets of People Who Are Successful	18
Chapter 9	What is Success?	20
Chapter 10	One Word to Define Success	22
Chapter 11	What Determines Success?	24
Chapter 12	An Accumulation of Wealth	26
Chapter 13	Success is Not Forever and Failure is Not Fatal	28
Chapter 14	Do Not Underestimate Your Skills	30
Chapter 15	The Most Important Ingredient for Your Success	32

Part 3: Why Do We Suffer?

Chapter 16	Why Do We Suffer?	36
Chapter 17	How to Get What You Want	38
Chapter 18	An Opportunity for Guaranteed Enlightenment	40
Chapter 19	Are You Guilty?	42
Chapter 20	Eliminating Worry	44
Chapter 21	Your Window of Perceptions and Why Do We Argue?	46
Chapter 22	How to Eliminate Self-Sabotaging Beliefs	48
Chapter 23	Everything is Relative	50

Part 4: A Secret to a Great Life

Chapter 24	Who Are You Not to Be?	54
Chapter 25	Life is About Creating Yourself	56
Chapter 26	How Successful People Deal with Failure	58
Chapter 27	What Does it Take to Be Attractive?	60
Chapter 28	How Much Do You Love Yourself?	62
Chapter 29	The Secret to a Great Life	64

Part 5: Are You a Natural Leader

Chapter 30	Are You a Natural Leader?	68
Chapter 31	The Power of a Team and Co-Operation	70
Chapter 32	Using Words with Good Purpose	72
Chapter 33	Personal Satisfaction at Work	74
Chapter 34	Helping is Not Always Good	76
Chapter 35	What is Your Greatness?	78
Chapter 36	Are You Busy Being Busy?	80

Part 6: Time Management & Decision Making

Chapter 37	Effective Decision Making	84
Chapter 38	How Much Do You Rely on Logic?	86
Chapter 39	Are there Bad Decisions?	88
Chapter 40	The Currency of Today	90
Chapter 41	Creating a Balanced Life	92
Chapter 42	The Value of an Hour	94
Chapter 43	The Slower You Go, The Faster You Will Get There	96
Chapter 44	Are You Living for the Future?	98

Part 7: The Best Source of Wealth

Chapter 45	Produce the Results You are Looking For	102
Chapter 46	What did You Miss Out on Today?	104
Chapter 47	The Power of Questions	106
Chapter 48	Ask and You Will Receive	108

Chapter 49	Excellence is Not an Act, But a Habit	110
Chapter 50	The Best Source of Wealth	112

Part 8: It Is Never Too Late

Chapter 51	You Make a Difference!	116
Chapter 52	Can One Person Change the World?	118
Chapter 53	It is Never Too Late	120
Conclusion	The Most Important Job You Do	122

References and Recommended Reading	*125*
About the Artist	*127*
About the Author	*128*
Thank You	*129*

FORWARD

by Cary Johnston

(*former London-based BBC reporter and current freelance journalist.*)

Some people are born into money. Some people are born into power. Most of us however just seem content to shrug our shoulders and settle for what little we appear to have, however unhappy that might make us feel. But is that really good enough…? Masha Malka doesn't think so.

She greets you with an air of quiet confidence and for someone so used to public speaking and dealing with the leaders of industry, it is a surprise to discover that Masha has a rather gentle voice and a disarming smile. Clearly, her power comes not from posturing, but from the knowledge that her tuition and methods have been proven to work. Only the occasional break in her accent gives a hint of her eastern European roots.

The young Masha grew up in the post Cold War atmosphere of a Soviet-controlled Ukraine, in a city called Kharkov, on the border with Russia. She may have had high ambitions for herself, but in the former Soviet Union, free and easy movement was hard to come by.

Not that Masha was desperate to leave. After all, the Soviet Union provided free education, free extra curricular activities and free summer camps! For a youngster, this was like heaven. But her parents, themselves modestly employed, could foresee the future workplace limitations, and while Masha left school at the age of 15 and went to a dance college for two years, her mother toiled with the necessary bureaucracy to allow her to take her daughter out of the country – she'd been asking the authorities for nine years. A Jewish family, their initial aim was to head for Israel.

Finally, in the late 80's atmosphere of Mikhael Gorbachev's perestroika era, permission was granted and Masha's parents were allowed to leave the Ukraine, taking their 17 year old daughter, 13 year old son and sick grandfather with them. The problem was, when you left the Soviet Union, you left with nothing.

The authorities stripped them of their citizenship and until their departure, Masha's mother wouldn't even let her play outside, for fear of reprisals from neighbours, such was the shame associated with abandoning the Soviet system. You were deemed to be an enemy of the state.

At the border, they were only allowed to take the equivalent of one hundred dollars each and were even denied a last group photo – no mementos, no chance of return and no one in the family able to speak anything other than Russian. They were now refugees and for Masha, this was to be the beginning of the dark time…

The family were first sent to Vienna; a normal procedure at the time. There, they would be processed and told which Western country might accept them. For three months, they were in limbo, but even in Vienna the culture shock was immense. Masha's mother once sent her to a supermarket to buy some jam. A bewildered Masha surveyed the twenty different jams on the shelf and experienced her first dose of cultural paralysis, spending the next two hours examining the different labels. After all, why didn't they make things easy and just produce one kind?

One day, on a visit to a public swimming pool, Masha saw a woman bathing topless and ran up to her to inform the poor lady that maybe she had lost her clothes and could she help her find them?

Eventually, the United States was chosen as their next destination, but adjusting to a new lifestyle was difficult, especially without a firm grasp of the English language. Her parents could only get cleaning jobs, so money was tight and the young Masha was sent to American High School. The shock of liberal dress codes and complete freedom of speech was out of this world. For her, it was like another planet!

But nonetheless, she persevered in her studies and although at first she found the English language difficult to master, she was exceptional at Mathematics – a universal language all of its own. Different part-time jobs followed to help make ends meet. Sales person, cashier, and assistant at the University of Miami, which at the time housed one of only two public scanners in the whole of the United States. For her, it felt like the greatest privilege and achievement to be in charge of using it!

But she had no idea what to do with her life, and while America seemed like the land of plenty, it can also be a lonely place for one raised in a totally different system. It seemed, especially in the go-getting atmosphere of the United States, that everyone else knew exactly what they wanted and where they were going. Culturally lost and professionally unsure, Masha had turned from being a confident outgoing individual, to an introverted and depressed individual, with little or no self-esteem.

It's here that the turning point came, when by chance she came across a life-coaching tape made by Brian Tracy (see credits) and discovered that self-esteem and the ability to be responsible for your own life, were the secrets to great success. By taking those seeds and with years of painstaking research, Masha not only learned to grow a new life for herself, but is now willing and able to share her discoveries with you, in the pages of this book.

It's not about forcing change, it's about being a catalyst for change. You can only help people who want to be helped, and Masha became an expert in guiding people to answer the questions they already knew the answers to, but were unwilling or unable to face. It's about encouragement. It's about striving to be where you want to be. It's about enjoying your life to the full.

Today, Masha's confidence (and smile!) comes from living the life she wants to live in southern Spain. Married with three children, she is still more than able to pursue her career on her terms. Her journey from hardship to happiness is proof that anyone is capable of positive change. So open your mind and let Masha show you how to make the most of your talents. Your new life starts here ...

INTRODUCTION FROM THE AUTHOR

Dear friend,

Where will you be 1 year from now?

Will you be doing the same things, going to the same places, spending time with the same people, wishing the same things, realizing that with each year that passes, those wishes will probably never materialize?

Or will you be moving rapidly towards the life of your dreams, having made the necessary changes in your mentality, having taken necessary action steps, feeling great about your future, about your progress and about yourself as a person? The choice is YOURS!

By buying this book you have already made a choice that puts you among a group of people who care about their future, their growth, and their overall happiness and fulfillment in life. Though I wish I could talk to you face to face, I am honored to do it through the words on these pages and I am grateful to you for helping me fulfill my purpose in life!

I have designed the book using Accelerated Learning Techniques and Neuro-Linguistic Programming to make it easy for you to read and assimilate the information, and more importantly, to apply it in your day-to-day life. There are 52 inspirational messages with an application/action step for each message. You can read and apply one a week for the duration of the year or you can use the book as a reference guide and consult it on specific topics as needed.

HOW you use the book is not as important as WHAT you do with the information in it. To make a real difference in your life requires not just an understanding of what would make it different but also consistent focused action.

Without taking up any more of your valuable time, let me thank you for buying The One Minute Coach™ and welcome you on an exciting journey of self-discovery and growth!

Your partner in success,

PART 1

FREEDOM TO BE WHO YOU ARE

CHAPTER 1

WHOSE LIFE ARE YOU LIVING?

"*Everything great was created starting with a decision – your new life is no exception*" – **Masha Malka**

Have you ever felt like you are living someone else's life? It is one of the worst feelings one can experience and most of us, at some point, do!

The first and most important step to living a fulfilling and authentic life that is totally and wonderfully YOURS is to realize that it's YOUR life and you deserve to live it on YOUR terms. The next step is to remember what life you are meant to live, to go back to 'who you really are' and let your passions and true personal desires surface again.

The process is easier for some than others but the benefits are well worth it! Some of the benefits of living YOUR life are:

- Life has meaning and purpose
- Your self-esteem shoots up
- You deal with life's obstacles effectively
- People just want to be with you
- You attract positivity into your life
- You feel fulfilled and happy

The benefits are many and cannot all be described in words but the main reason for living YOUR life is this: YOU DESERVE TO!

I myself have been in the darkness of not knowing 'who I am' and 'what I am meant to do' as well as experiencing the fulfillment of living a life of purpose. I have made the journey and I have seen others do it. Now, it is YOUR turn. I believe that every one of us deserves to live an authentic life – a fulfilling and happy life. I made it my purpose to help as many people as I can to achieve that.

Action Steps

1. Start a journal to follow your progress as you go through this book.
2. Decide on the time of the day that you will spend focusing on yourself – reading, writing, reflecting, applying what you learn, and anything else that helps you grow and move in the direction you want to go.

CHAPTER 2

THE 'IMPOSSIBLE' IS OFTEN THE UNTRIED

"*What is now proved was once impossible.*" – **William Blake**, (1757–1827 British poet and artist)

"*If you deliberately plan on being less than you are capable of being, then I warn you that you'll be unhappy for the rest of your life.*" – **Abraham H. Maslow**, (1908–1970 American psychologist)

Do you believe it is possible for you to become fulfilled and successful in all areas of your life?

You might know an unforgettable example of making the impossible possible, achieved by **Roger Bannister** on May 6th 1954. For centuries before that date it was considered humanly impossible to run a mile in under 4 minutes. There was a widespread belief that if you did, your heart would explode!

Roger Bannister believed something different and proved to the world that what was considered to be impossible was not so. The amazing fact is not just that Mr. Bannister was able to run a mile in less than 4 minutes but that just one year later 37 other people around the world followed his example and within two years 300 runners managed to break the previously 'impossible' record!

Why?

Because whatever you believe becomes your self-fulfilling prophecy. If you believe it is impossible for you to become successful and fulfilled in all areas of your life, it is very unlikely that you will. However, if you see someone in the same position as you, who has 'made it' and you change your belief system because of that example, you will open the door to the great possibility of becoming and getting all that you want in life.

Action Steps

1. Remind yourself daily that if you desire something with all your heart and soul, it is because you are meant to have it. As one of the wisest persons who ever lived, **Rebbe Nachman of Breslov** (1772–1810), points out: "Always remember, you are never given an obstacle you cannot overcome."
2. Create an unshakable belief in your ability to reach your goals. When you follow your dreams and believe you can reach them, everything in life supports you. Even the obstacles you come across along the way are there to teach you and ultimately help you get where you want to be.

CHAPTER 3

IF THEY CAN DO IT, SO CAN YOU!

"*One must have the adventurous daring to accept oneself as a bundle of possibilities and undertake the most interesting game in the world – making the most of one's best.*" – **Harry Emerson Fosdick**, (1878–1969 American Baptist Pastor)

"*To be fully alive is to feel that everything is possible.*" – **Eric Hoffer**, (1902–1983 American writer)

Are you making the most of your best?

When **Pete Sampras'** school-mates were out playing and socializing, Pete practiced his tennis. Years later, when Pete was already the top tennis player in the world, he did things differently again. He took his whole game apart in order to raise himself to a new level. It paid off. He went on to beat the then record of 12 Grand Slam Singles titles.

When everyone around **Bill Gates** was skeptical about the widespread usage of computers, Bill envisaged a PC in every home. He took appropriate actions based on his vision and the rest is history.

Celine Dion dreamt of being an internationally acclaimed singer from the age of five.

Jim Carrey didn't let the reality of being a factory floor cleaner deter him from becoming the comedian he wanted to be. In fact he wrote himself a cheque for $20 million and carried it around with him in his wallet. In 1995, he was offered that same amount for his role in the movie The Cable Guy!

What is it that these people have in common that enabled them to do what they did?

What enabled them to stand out from the crowd?

How can you do the same?

If they Can Do It, So Can You! | **7**

Action Steps

1. The first and most important thing you have to do is BELIEVE that what you want to achieve is possible!
2. Learn as much as you can in that area and take consistent focused action until you achieve it.

CHAPTER 4

ARE YOU STARVING YOUR SOUL?

"*The level of success and fulfillment you enjoy in your life is the result of how well you contribute to your purpose.*" – **Masha Malka**

What is your purpose in life? Is it important to stop and think about it?

I believe it is. Because having a clear purpose in life, making a difference in the lives of others happens to be one of the greatest human hungers! If you don't have a clear purpose, you are starving your soul!

According to **Robin Sharma**, author of the bestselling book The Monk Who Sold His Ferrari, people have a deep inner need to be a part of something larger than themselves. Whether we are speaking of the CEO or the shipping clerk, every human being needs to feel that he or she is making some sort of contribution.

Richard J. Leider has made it his purpose to help others discover theirs. In his book The Power of Purpose he states: "Purpose is the conscious choice of what, where, and how to make a positive contribution to our world. It is the theme, quality, or passion we choose to center our lives around."

Re-discovering what makes you tick – what you are passionate about, is essential to living the life you desire and deserve! If what you do on a daily basis is not aligned with your talents, passion and purpose in life, you will not be very eager to get up in the morning.

"*If your life is worth living, it is worth living with purpose!*" – **Masha Malka**

Action Steps

If you don't have a compelling reason to get up in the morning, a purpose that drives you to do what you do, then make it your primary goal to find out what it is. Here are some steps that will help you with your discovery:

1. Pay attention to what you are passionate about – passion and purpose go hand in hand.
2. Imagine yourself being very old and analyzing your life. What achievements are you most proud of?
3. Finally, ask yourself this powerful question: "If I had all the money and time I needed and could do anything knowing without a doubt that I would succeed what would I do?"

Enjoy the process and remember that it is never too early or too late to start living a life of purpose. Most likely you have been doing it for years without even realizing it!

CHAPTER 5

WHAT FULFILLS YOU?

"*People who live happy and fulfilling lives are those who know what they want and do not settle for anything less than that!*" – **Masha Malka**

What fulfillment means to you is intensely personal. When people first think about it, they might focus on outward measures of success, a great job, enough money, or a certain lifestyle. But if you focus deeper, you will realize that true fulfillment is not about having more. It is not about what fills your pockets or closets, it is about what fills your heart and your soul.

A fulfilling life is a valued life. What are your top values? Are they being honored?

Sorting out your values is a way of sorting out life choices because when the choices honor your values, life is more satisfying and seems almost effortless.

Also, though achieving a certain goal can be very fulfilling, you often find that this kind of fulfillment is not the finish line. At its deepest level it is about finding and experiencing a life of purpose; it is about living by your values.

It is about reaching one's full potential.

Action Steps

1. Most people live their lives caught up in the daily routine, never stopping and asking themselves: "What is my purpose?" "What are my core values?" "What really fulfills me?" If you have never thought about purpose and values before, then the first step is to do just that. Spend time with yourself thinking about your life. Think about where you are going and what makes you really happy.
2. Realize that there is no right or wrong purpose or right or wrong set of values; there is only YOUR purpose and YOUR set of values – the ones that feel right to your heart!

CHAPTER 6

FREEDOM TO BE WHO YOU ARE

"Don't say "If I could, I would." Say instead "If I can, I will." – **Jim Rohn**, *(Motivational Coach).*

In pre-school the children were busy drawing pictures. As the teacher walked around the tables, she asked one of the boys named Harry, what he was drawing.

"I am drawing God!" he replied.

"You can't draw God… nobody knows what he looks like!" exclaimed the teacher. "They will after I finish!" replied Harry.

As children, we do not let other people's opinions (and even accepted facts) influence our actions. Unfortunately, as we grow up, we become very dependent on what others think; on what is considered 'right' and what is considered 'wrong'. Many of us even choose our careers and our life partners depending on how it will be accepted by everyone around us.

I say, you only have one life to live – YOUR life! Do not let human dependency for approval and acceptance affect you. Do not settle for a comfortable existence when you deserve a wonderful life of purpose and fulfilment!

Action Steps

1. What can you do to live a life of purpose and fulfilment? Just one thing – commit to yourself (if you haven't done so yet) that you will not settle for anything less than that.
2. When you allow yourself to be who you are, you automatically allow others to do the same.
3. You can give this gift of personal freedom to yourself and others. All you need is the courage to live your life on your terms!

CHAPTER 7

IT ALL COMES DOWN TO FAITH

Someone once told me that if you have $100.000 in the bank no one ever tells you how to live your life! Well, maybe some people still tell you, but it is done on a different level and not as often as if you were struggling financially. Why is success mainly measured by how much money you have? It is no wonder that so many people give up on their dreams in pursuit of financial stability and approval from others!

No one likes to be told what to do and how to do it. We like the approval of others, especially our loved ones, so we give up on what is important to us and become part of the masses, doing 'what works,' what's been done before and what more or less guarantees a pay check.

Often there is money in your bank, but what about your heart? Is it content; is it full of life and passion, full of love and appreciation, full of anticipation of what the next day will bring? Is the next day of your life truly YOURS?

Do not misunderstand me; there is nothing wrong with wanting to have money and striving for financial stability. In fact, it is an important part of your overall success. The point I am making is that while working on creating wealth, remember to take care of all your other needs as well.

In order to have something that you do not currently have in your life, you first have to become the kind of person who attracts whatever you want into your life. Be it the kind of partner that you want, be it wealth, certain types of friends, a healthy body, or just peace of mind.

Yes, at times it seems like a very slow process. We all want results NOW, we want immediate gratification. We want what can be measured with our physical senses.

So what is the solution? Well, it all comes down to FAITH. To live the life of your dreams – the life that is truly YOURS – it is essential to have faith in your dreams, in yourself and in the Universe!

Action Steps

1. When you know exactly what you want, do all that you can to become the kind of person who will attract it. If you are looking for a fulfilling relationship, immerse yourself in the information and thoughts on what makes such a relationship possible.
2. The same goes for wealth. To attract wealth, raise your "wealth conscience" – study money, read about money, find out what wealthy people think about and do, when it comes to money. Before you know it, great people, wealth, health, and everything else you constantly focus on will manifest into your life and STAY there!

PART 2

THE SECRETS OF PEOPLE WHO ARE SUCCESSFUL

CHAPTER 8

THE SECRETS OF PEOPLE WHO ARE SUCCESSFUL

"The successful person makes a habit of doing what the failing person doesn't like to do." – **Thomas Edison**, (1847–1931 American inventor and businessman)

What do successful people know, think, believe and do that the rest do not? What are the secrets of people who are successful?

Fortunately, there are no secrets! There is a certain set of beliefs, habits, and a particular attitude of mind that anyone can learn and make their own – in the process ATTRACTING success in all areas of their lives. I have studied success and successful people for many years and have concluded that some of the aspects they have in common are:

- They know what they want!
- They are usually very passionate about what they do.
- They have clear visions as to where they are going.
- They have clearly defined values by which they live and base their decisions.
- They have powerful winning habits.
- They have a positive outlook on life.
- They ask many questions and enjoy learning.
- Time is their most valuable commodity and they spend it wisely.
- They understand and accept themselves as they are!

Action Steps

If you haven't done so already, start a SUCCESS JOURNAL. Every night, before you go to sleep, write down the answers to the following 3 questions:

1. What am I grateful for today?
2. What new empowering things did I learn today?
3. What exciting new ideas do I have?

Every morning start your day with reading last night's entries in your success journal. Then add to it your goals for the day. And remember, the main thing that separates successful people from the rest is that they actually take action rather than just reading or thinking about taking it!

CHAPTER 9

WHAT IS SUCCESS?

Are you rushing through your days, working hard to achieve YOUR success or SOMEONE ELSE'S? Sometimes we are on autopilot, doing things because we feel we have to, because we feel it is our duty, yet, not really going anywhere...

Here is a story that might inspire you to stop and think about what you REALLY want:

It was a beautiful Friday afternoon and a wealthy businessman decided to take a trip on a small fishing boat guided by a young fisherman. The sun was glistening on the sea and the wealthy man took it upon himself to give the youngster some advice, as the boat gently moved away from the harbor.

"Son," said the wealthy businessman. "I can teach you the secrets of success, if you'll only listen carefully." "OK," smiled the young fisherman, as he cleaned the morning's catch.

Although a bit surprised by the young man's casual manner, the businessman began his lesson. "Now listen. The first thing you need to do is double your prices! You have a clean boat and by now you must have a good idea where the fattest fish are."

"Why would I want to do that?" replied the young fisherman, as he casually watched two crabs scampering by in the shallow waters.

The businessman could feel his irritation rising as he replied: "Because then you will have lots of money to buy more boats and attract more tourists and catch more fish. You'll soon have a fleet of boats!"

"But why would I want to do that?" the young fisherman asked as he lay back to soak up the gentle rays of the afternoon sun.

By now the businessman had reached the end of his tether: "Because then you will become rich and you can hire people to do your work while you spend your days fishing and relaxing in the sun!"

"Ah" the young fisherman nodded sagely. "That sounds wonderful!"

Action Steps

1. Ask yourself: 'Am I successful?' If 'yes' then 'What makes me successful?' If 'no,' 'What is missing in my life to make me feel successful?' Remember, success is just a FEELING, and it is up to you to decide what you need to do to experience that feeling, or under what circumstances you will ALLOW yourself to experience the feeling of success?
2. Here is another 'secret' of successful people. First, FEEL successful and then success will follow!

CHAPTER 10

ONE WORD TO DEFINE SUCCESS

"*Success isn't something you chase. It is something you have to put forth the effort for constantly, then maybe it'll come when you least expect it.*" – **Michael Jordan** (professional basketball player)

"*A great attitude is not the result of success; success is the result of a great attitude.*" – **Earl Nightingale** (1921–1989 entrepreneur, producer and publisher)

Can you define success? If you could use just one word to define success, what would it be?

When I ask my workshop participants and my coaching clients to define success the answers are usually different. So the one word that I would use to describe success is PERSONAL – it means different things to different people. Here is my definition of success:

I feel successful when I live my days consistent with my values, take action steps towards my goals and dreams, and when I make a difference in someone's life. I also believe that the ultimate measure of success is how good you feel about yourself on a regular basis!

I once asked one of my clients, world famous Poker Champion Paul Zimbler, what his definition of success was and here is what he shared with me:

> Success is achieving the best you can do
> Being honest, committed, hardworking, and true.
> Don't dwell in the past, look forward not back
> Give yourself chances others will lack.
>
> Anyone can make mistakes on the way
> Success is learning that errors can pay.
> Dream without limit, plan without fear
> Before you expect it, the future is here.
> Reach for the sky, aim for the sun,
> Achievers will finish a job once begun.

Action Steps

1. Write down your own definition of success. Unless you are very clear about what you are striving to achieve, how can you know when you've achieved it?
2. Find out what success means to the important people in your life. It will help you understand them better and assist them in achieving it.

CHAPTER 11

WHAT DETERMINES SUCCESS?

"*For every difficulty that supposedly stops a person from succeeding there are thousands who have had it a lot worse and have succeeded anyway. So can you.*" – **Brian Tracy** (self-development guru and author)

Are you predisposed to be successful or is it learnable? Let me share with you examples from history about people who didn't start as well as they finished.

One of the most influential figures of our millennium, **Thomas Edison**, didn't learn to talk until the age of four, had a learning disorder and has said later on in his life "My father thought I was stupid and I almost decided I must be a dunce."

Albert Einstein, whose name and image became a representation of supernormal intelligence, was dyslexic and had a very slow childhood development. His Greek teacher told him "You will never amount to anything." He was expelled from high school and failed his college entrance exam.

French post-impressionist painter **Paul Gauguin**, who helped form the basis of modern art, only began painting because he failed as a stockbroker.

The renowned French mathematical physicist **Henri Poincare** did very poorly on his IQ test and was proclaimed an 'imbecile.'

Rodgers and **Hammerstein's** first collaboration was so disastrous that they didn't work again for years. (They both went on to create several outstanding musical productions).

Walt Disney was fired by a newspaper editor because he lacked "good creative ideas."

Beethoven's music teacher told him he was "hopeless as a composer."

So what determines success? It is your mindset! Your set of beliefs and views about yourself and about life, that are fortunately learnable and changeable.

Action Steps

1. To be successful, you need to study success and what successful people do – their mindsets. In Neuro-Linguistic Programming terms it is called 'modelling'. Start noticing people around you who are successful as well as people who are famous for their success. What determines THEIR success? What determines YOUR success?
2. The more you think and analyze success, the more of it you will attract in your life – because what you focus on is what you get.

CHAPTER 12

AN ACCUMULATION OF WEALTH

"*Some day, in years to come, you will be wrestling with the great temptation, or trembling under the great sorrow of your life. But the real struggle is here, now, in these quiet weeks. Now it is being decided whether, in the day of your supreme sorrow or temptation, you shall miserably fail or gloriously conquer. Character cannot be made except by a steady, long continued process.*"
– **Phillips Brooks** (1835–1893 American Episcopal Bishop)

What does it take to become wealthy? To become successful? To become wise and knowledgeable?

Brian Tracy, a self-development guru whom I greatly admire, says that one of the best success principles of all is called The Law of Accumulation. This law states that 'Everything great and worthwhile in human life is an accumulation of hundreds and sometimes thousands of tiny efforts and sacrifices that nobody ever sees or appreciates.' It says that everything accumulates over time. That you have to put in many tiny efforts that nobody sees or appreciates before you achieve anything worthwhile. It's like a snowball. A snowball starts very small, but it grows as it adds millions and millions of tiny snowflakes and continues to grow as it gathers momentum.

Be conscious of the fact that everything that you do counts! A person who has a great life, by the law of accumulation, is a person who's accumulated far more credits on the credit side than debits on the debit side. What do I mean by that? Well, if what you are doing is not moving you towards your goals, then it's moving you away from your goals.

Nothing is neutral. You are either moving towards the things that you want to accomplish in life – the person you want to be and the wealth you want to accumulate – or you are moving away from it. As one, very successful, friend of mine likes to say: *"It took me 15 years of hard work to achieve an overnight success!"*

Action Steps

1. The most important action step here is to actually TAKE ACTION! However small it is, if it moves you in the right direction, just do it. If you have a dream, take at least one action step towards it in the next half hour – it will make you feel empowered and in control.
2. Then, do something everyday, keep your eyes on the destination and you WILL get there!

CHAPTER 13

SUCCESS IS NOT FOREVER AND FAILURE IS NOT FATAL

"*Don't get a big head when you win or get too down in the dumps when you lose. Keep things in perspective. Success is not forever, and failure isn't fatal.*" – **Don Shula**

How do you stay level-headed and calm when stress (both positive and negative) seems to be a constant in your life?

To answer this question, I would first point out that a certain level of stress is actually good for you; it is when it gets out of hand that it starts interfering with the way you function and how you react to this world. When your energies are channeled on mulling over what happened in the past or stressing out about the future, you cannot produce the kind of results you are capable of producing.

So what is the solution?

Don Shula, who is described as the most winning coach in NFL history, had a 24-HOUR RULE to deal with the stresses of winning or losing a game. He allowed himself and his players a maximum of 24 hours after a football game to celebrate a victory or grief over a defeat. During that time, everyone was encouraged to experience the thrill of victory or the agony of defeat as deeply as possible, while learning as much as they could from that same experience.

Once the 24-hour deadline had passed, they put it behind them and focused their energies on preparing for the next opponent.

Success is Not Forever and Failure is Not Fatal | **29**

> ## Action Steps
>
> 1. The next time you find yourself filled with despair over loss or failure or celebrating a great achievement, apply Shula's 24-hour rule – give yourself a 24 hour deadline to deal with it and then get on with your life.
> 2. By the way, Hall of Fame Coach, Shula is the only coach to guide a team (the Miami Dolphins) through an undefeated NFL season (17-0 in 1972)! Who knows, maybe applying his rule will help YOU have an undefeated life! And if it doesn't...well, you have 24 hours to get over it!

CHAPTER 14

DO NOT UNDERESTIMATE YOUR SKILLS

Do you know what you are worth? Most people tend to underestimate their skills and undercharge their services. The following is a parable which I believe we can all learn from...

There was once a wealthy man who owned a wonderful luxury steamship, but after a particularly long and difficult journey, the engine failed and no one could get it working again. Several well known mechanics and engineers from across the land were summoned to try to fix the engine, but one by one they failed. Finally, when the wealthy man had nearly given up, word arrived that a wise old ship maker might be able to help, but at a hefty price. The wealthy man agreed at once...

And so it came to pass that the old man, who looked like he might be one hundred years old, shuffled slowly on board, carrying a large bag of old tools.

As the steamship owner looked on with suspicion, the old man began to peer at the large network of pipes leading to and from the engine, occasionally placing his hand upon the pipes to test for warmth.

Finally, and without a word, the old man reached into his bag and pulled out a small hammer. He gently tapped against one of the pipes. Instantly, the sound of steam rushing through the pipes could be heard and the engine lurched into life as he carefully put his hammer away.

When the wealthy man asked for the bill, it came to ten thousand dollars.

"What?!" exclaimed the wealthy owner. "You hardly did anything at all! I shall have my lawyers take you to court for malpractice!"

Without a word, the old ship maker took out a pencil and scrawled something onto a ragged piece of paper he'd pulled from his pocket. The wealthy man smiled as he read it and apologized to the old man for his rude behavior.

The note read:
For tapping with a hammer..........................$1
For knowing where to tap............................$9999

Action Steps

1. Remember, you are a unique human being with a unique combination of skills, knowledge and experience that no one else possesses.
2. You can never earn in the outside world more than you can earn in your own mind. If you want to earn more money, first become very comfortable with the new sum in your mind and then you will be able to attract it into your life.
3. Know your worth and others will do the same in return.

CHAPTER 15

THE MOST IMPORTANT INGREDIENT FOR YOUR SUCCESS

"*Calm self-confidence is as far from conceit as the desire to earn a decent living is remote from greed.*" – **Channing Pollock** (1880–1946 American playwright, critic and writer)

"*To have that sense of one's intrinsic worth which constitutes self-respect is potentially to have everything.*" – **Joan Didion** (American writer, journalist, and essayist)

What would you say is the most important ingredient for overall success?

I believe it is self-confidence and a high level of self-esteem. You can only achieve your goals and attract success when you feel you deserve to have, to do, or to be what you want. You feel you deserve it all when your self-esteem is high.

The formula is simple: raise your self-esteem and a new level of success follows! To have more confidence and self-esteem within days, just follow the 5 action steps below.

Action Steps

1. Anthony Robbins, an achievement guru, suggests you stop analyzing yourself and focus on how you can contribute to others.
2. He also encourages controlling your mental focus. The fastest way to change what you're focusing on, says Robbins, is to change the questions you're asking yourself. For example, change statements such as "What happens if I fail at this?" or "Why do I always screw these things up?" to "What's the best way to get this done now?" or better yet "What's the best way to get this done and enjoy the process?"
3. Change your core beliefs. Change from "I've never done it before so I don't see how I could do it today" to "If I can imagine it, I can achieve it!"
4. Recall 5 of your greatest successes and write a paragraph in your success / gratitude journal describing each one. Use these examples to remind yourself that you can always find a way!
5. Take good care of yourself regularly. Because, when you take care of yourself – your growth, your happiness and self-fulfillment – you inevitably take care of the world and the people around you; their happiness and their future!

CHAPTER 16

WHY DO WE SUFFER?

"*We suffer less when we let go of planning ahead to feel poorly."*
- Hale Dwoskin

I believe that most of our suffering is caused by our own perceptions! In his best-selling book, The Sedona Method, Hale Dwoskin points out that the reason problems appear to persist through time, is that whenever they're not here in this moment we go looking for them.

We tend to filter our experiences based on the belief that we have a particular problem, unconsciously censoring anything from our awareness that doesn't support that belief, including the fact that the problem is not here NOW. Here is an interesting story that illustrates this point.

> Two monks were wandering through the woods one day when they came upon a beautiful young woman standing on the banks of a flooded stream. She clearly wanted to cross to the other side without ruining her dignity and asked the monks if they could help. However, because he had sworn a vow of chastity, the younger monk ignored her pleas and crossed the stream without her.
>
> But, the older monk proceeded to gather her up in his arms and carried her across the stream where he gently lowered her to the ground, safe and dry. She thanked him and the two monks continued on their way.
>
> However, the younger monk was perturbed by the incident and ran it over again and again in his mind. How dare the older monk act in that way? Did his vow of chastity mean nothing to him? The more the young monk thought about what he had seen, the angrier he became. After all, if HE had done such a thing he would have been thrown out of the order. This is appalling and shameful, he thought. The more he thought about it, the worse it seemed.
>
> He looked over at the older monk to see if he was at least showing remorse for what he had done, but the man seemed as serene and peaceful as ever. Finally, the young monk could stand it no longer. "How could you do that?!" he demanded. "How could you even look at that woman, let alone pick her up and carry her? Have you forgotten your vow of chastity?"
>
> The older monk looked surprised, then smiled with great kindness in his eyes: "I am no longer carrying her my brother," and said. "Are you?"

Action Steps

1. Every time you want to analyze a problem, think of it as though it was in the PAST. Do not try to understand why it happened to you unless you are planning to experience it again in the future.
2. Remember, whatever you focus on is what you get again and again and again. Instead of focusing on what is wrong and why, focus on what is right and on what you WANT to experience today and in the future.

CHAPTER 17

HOW TO GET WHAT YOU WANT

"*The greatest discovery of my generation is that human beings can alter their lives by altering their attitudes of mind.*" – **William James** (1842–1910 pioneering American psychologist and philosopher)

"*You have powers you never dreamed of. You can do things you never thought you could do. There are no limitations in what you can do except the limitations of your own mind.*" – **Darwin P. Kingsley** (1906–1930 American business leader)

Have you ever found yourself wondering why someone who is not as smart, not as good looking, not as creative, not as connected, not nearly as 'good a person' as you, seems to have it all…while you, who seems to give, give, give, and do, do, do, are still struggling? Or maybe you heard someone else say that?

The answer is simple; what one person possesses and the other doesn't, has nothing to do with what that person has or does…it concerns that person's MINDSET. The mindset is the belief system that people operate with, determining what they experience, what they do, what they have and who they are as people.

For you to attract money, good health, loving relationships, or anything else you desire, you have to develop a mindset that will allow your desires to flow freely into your life.

Action Steps

1. The best way to develop a mindset that allows you to have what you want is to study the mindsets of people who already have what you want.
2. Changing your thoughts and beliefs changes your life! Be positive, optimistic and grateful. Rather than worry and attract negative events, project into the future what you WANT to experience.
3. Be congruent. Align all your thoughts, beliefs and actions in the direction you want to go. For example, if you want to be wealthy but think that money is dirty or that rich people are selfish, then you are not congruent.
4. Finally, know deep in your heart that you deserve to have all that your heart desires! Be comfortable with having it in your mind first and the reality will follow shortly.

CHAPTER 18

AN OPPORTUNITY FOR GUARANTEED ENLIGHTENMENT

"*You gain strength, courage and confidence by every experience in which you really stop to look fear in the face. You must do the thing you think you cannot do.*" – **Eleanor Roosevelt** (1884–1962 Former American First Lady)

"*Courage is not the absence of fear, but rather the judgment that something else is more important than one's fear.*" – **Ambrose Redmoon** (1933–1996 American writer and rock music manager)

What is your greatest fear? Are you ready to let it go?

There is a story that in ancient Tibet, all the monks would gather together once every hundred years and be given an opportunity for guaranteed enlightenment – all they had to do was walk through the Room of a Thousand Demons and come out alive.

The Room of a Thousand Demons was a pitch-black room filled with a thousand demons who would appear to you in the guise of your biggest and worst fears: spiders, snakes, sheer precipices – whatever they sensed would fill your heart with terror. The only rules were that once you entered no one could come in and rescue you and it was impossible to leave by the door you went in.

For those few brave souls who dared to face their fears in pursuit of happiness, success and enlightenment, there was one crucial piece of advice:

"No matter what you see, hear, think or feel, keep moving. If you keep your feet moving, you will eventually get to where it is you want to go!"

Action Steps

1. Identify something you've wanted to do for a long time but feel too afraid to do. Something that you possibly keep postponing, finding very good reasons for not doing, yet all the time getting that feeling in your gut that this is something that needs to be done. It could be calling someone, sharing something, speaking in public, leaving your job, starting a new career...YOU KNOW what it is!
2. Remember, nothing comes without a price and the price for not doing what needs to be done is much higher than actually doing it!
3. Identify what it is you fear and just do it. Your courage will liberate, empower, and enlighten you!

CHAPTER 19

ARE YOU GUILTY?

"Lack of forgiveness causes almost all of our self-sabotaging behavior." – **Mark Victor Hansen** (American motivational speaker, trainer and author)

Let's talk about overcoming feelings of GUILT and SHAME – those seductive robbers of our freedom, inner peace of mind and happiness.

Feelings of guilt and shame are self-infused and cause us much unnecessary suffering. According to **Hale Dwoskin**, author of one of my favorite books The Sedona Method, guilt is the feeling of remorse that follows a perceived wrongdoing; shame is a painful emotion resulting from an awareness of inadequacy or guilt. While it is possible to feel guilt without shame, we cannot feel shame without guilt.

Don't let any one make you feel guilty! Including, or should I say, especially, yourself!

Negative people with low-self esteems tend to do it to others because it gives them a false sense of superiority. In fact, it only contributes to their low self-esteem as well as yours. Remember, nobody can make you feel anything unless you let them! Guilt and shame do nothing except make what you did worse for yourself and others.

Action Steps

1. Forgive yourself. You are not a bad person because you did something that made you feel guilty. If you were you wouldn't feel guilty about it.
2. Realize that feeling guilty or shameful is your way of punishing yourself for what you did or thinking that it will prevent future recurrence of the event. Nothing can be further from reality because by holding in your mind and constantly replaying the event that made you feel guilty, you make it a lot more possible to happen again.
3. Remember what we visualize and think about – we manifest. At the end we never feel as though we've been sufficiently punished anyway. If you've been holding onto feelings of guilt or shame, it is time to let go of these destructive feelings. They are just feelings; they are not who you are. Learn from them, let them go, and move on!
4. If you made a mistake, acknowledge it, apologize for it, learn from it, let go and be happy! It is your right!

CHAPTER 20

ELIMINATING WORRY

"*Worry does not empty tomorrow of sorrow – it empties today of strength*" – **Carrie Ten Bloom** (best-selling author)

"*When I look back on all these worries I remember the story of the old man who said on his deathbed that he had a lot of trouble in his life, most of which had never happened.*" – **Sir Winston Churchill** (1874–1965 UK Prime Minister)

The reason why worry kills more people than work is that more people worry than work. – **Robert Frost** (1875–1963 American Poet)

"*Stop the mindless wishing that things would be different. Rather than wasting time and emotional and spiritual energy in explaining why we don't have what we want, we can start to pursue other ways to get it.*" – **Greg Anderson** (American writer and cancer survivor)

One of the worst energy and time wasters – WORRY – is a big part of many people's lives. Ask yourself:

- "Do I worry a lot?"
- "What happens when I worry?"
- "What is worrying me?"

Worrying is a process of thinking and visualizing a non-desirable outcome. Most likely you already know that it is a dangerous process, since we don't want to focus on what we don't want to experience. So what to do?

Action Steps

1. To eliminate worry, first identify the worst possible outcome of any particular situation and decide how you would deal with it.
2. Then quickly change the image to exactly what you want to happen and keep THAT image in your head.

CHAPTER 21

YOUR WINDOW OF PERCEPTIONS AND WHY DO WE ARGUE?

If you have ever tried to convince someone of something that made perfect sense to you but not to that person, it is because of the difference in your belief systems.

Here is an interesting story told by the legendary psychologist, **Abraham Maslow:**

> A psychiatrist was treating a patient who believed that he was a corpse. The psychiatrist used every cognitive approach to convince the man that he was indeed alive, all to no avail.
>
> In a moment of revelation, the psychiatrist asked the man, "Do you believe that corpses bleed?" the patient replied: "That's ridiculous! Of course corpses don't bleed."
>
> After asking permission, the psychiatrist pricked the patient's finger, producing a drop of red blood. At that moment, the psychiatrist thought that a moment of enlightenment was forthcoming. However, the patient looked at his finger with astonishment and exclaimed: "I'll be damned, corpses do bleed!"

Your beliefs shape your experiences and the way you see the world. They determine your decisions, how you feel about things, how you react to things and ultimately the direction you take in life.

Imagine you are in a tall tower with millions of windows that have very different views. Your beliefs will determine through which window you will choose to view the world outside.

This is not just important to understand why and how you experience YOUR life, but also to understand that different people sit at different windows and view different things. What is true to you from your window might not be so for another person.

Action Steps

1. Keep the above in mind next time someone is trying to force their point of view on you or you on them.
2. Unless you are willing to adopt or understand each other's belief systems and look at the situation at hand from 'the same window' you will just get frustrated trying to understand something that doesn't exist in your window of perceptions.

CHAPTER 22

HOW TO ELIMINATE SELF-SABOTAGING BELIEFS

"*Our only limitations are those which we set up in our minds or permit others to establish for us.*" – **Elizabeth Arden** (1878–1966 Canadian businesswoman)

Let's talk about, what is probably your worst enemy when it comes to success – SELF-SABOTAGE.

According to **Anthony Robbins**, a leading authority on self-development and peak performance, anything we do, including "self-sabotage," we do with positive intent. That means that our brain at some level, conscious or unconscious, is always trying to benefit us in some way through its actions.

For example, if you tried to lose weight in the past unsuccessfully, you might have noticed that as soon as you reached a certain weight, something would trigger you to gain it all back. Understand that in cases like that, your brain is not trying to hurt you.

In fact, your brain may simply be trying to protect you from succeeding and putting yourself in the position of needing to continue doing so; i.e. your fear of success may actually be protecting you from a situation where you may ultimately feel rejected.

I believe we all have self-sabotaging beliefs in certain areas of our lives – it might be money, relationships, weight issues, or success in general.

WHY we sabotage ourselves is not as important to understand (you might spend years trying to find out and it will only cause low self-esteem) as learning HOW to eliminate self-sabotaging beliefs.

Action Steps

1. Identify in what areas of your life you might be sabotaging yourself.
2. Do everything in your power to feel good because your brain is trying to help you avoid pain and gain pleasure.
3. Interrupt the old pattern. There are many different techniques you can use. Check some on page 62 (Life is About Creating Yourself). I would also recommend reading Personal Power II by Anthony Robbins.
4. Rehearse achieving the success you want and feel the pleasure of succeeding until it becomes your new empowering habit.

CHAPTER 23

EVERYTHING IS RELATIVE

When you think one situation is bad, that is because you are comparing it to something you perceive is better. Let's look at this example:

Imagine you have a daughter who recently left for college. She is only 19 years old and it is the first time she has been away from home. You haven't heard from her in a while and suddenly the long-awaited letter arrives:

Dear Mum and Dad,

Apologies for taking so long to write, but my writing utensils were destroyed in the fire at my apartment. I am out of the hospital and the doctor says that I should be able to lead a normal healthy life.

A handsome young man called Pete saved me from the fire and kindly offered to share his apartment with me. He is very kind and polite and from a good family, so I think you'll approve when I tell you that we got married last week.

I know you'll be even more excited when I tell you that you are going to be grandparents very soon!

Actually there wasn't a fire, I haven't been in hospital, I'm not married and I'm not pregnant, but I did fail my biology exam and I just wanted to make sure that when I told you, you put it in proper perspective.

Love,
Your daughter.

When my 6-year-old daughter lost a pair of white shoes at the pool, she optimistically came to me and said, "Isn't it great, Mommy, that I didn't lose my pink shoes as well!"

Most young children have an inborn sense of optimism and positive expectations in life. That is because they haven't yet learned how to be negative.

I believe that things can always be better and they can always be worse but whatever happens to us at this moment is exactly what should happen and it is for the best!

Everything is Relative | **51**

Action Steps

Make a conscious effort to enjoy each moment, stay positive and expect the best in life. Before you know it, it will become another one of your positive habits!

CHAPTER 24

WHO ARE YOU NOT TO BE?

"When one door of happiness closes, another opens; but often we look so long at the closed door that we do not see the one which has been opened for us." – **Helen Keller**, (1880-1968 deaf blind American author, activist and lecturer)

It is amazing how many people feel they don't deserve to be happy, don't deserve to have the best, don't deserve to BE the best, don't deserve to have it all! Many settle for second best, many get stuck in the comfort zone, in the familiar. They don't want to 'rock the boat'. Second best plus security is a lot more important to them than going for the life of their dreams.

Why?

To answer' that question, let me share with you one of my favorite poems that **Marianne Williamson**, spiritual activist, author, and lecturer, wrote for **Nelson Mandela's** 1994 inauguration speech as president of South Africa:

A Return for Love

Our deepest fear is not that we are inadequate.
Our deepest fear is that we are powerful beyond measure.
It is our light, not our darkness, that most frightens us.
We ask ourselves:
Who am I to be brilliant, gorgeous, talented and fabulous?
Actually who are you not to be?
You are a child of God.
Your playing small doesn't serve the world.
There is nothing enlightened about shrinking so that other people won't feel insecure around you.
We are born to manifest the glory of God that is within us.
It is not just in some of us; it's in everyone.
And as we let our own light shine, we unconsciously give other people permission to do the same.
As we are liberated from our own fear
our presence automatically liberates others.

Action Steps

1. Make a decision today that you deserve to live your life in a way that makes YOU happy. The rewards for this one decision are greater than you could ever imagine!
2. Choose today and for the rest of your life not to settle for second best because it is convenient, comfortable or secure. If you do that, you might always wonder where you could have ended up if you really did go for your dreams!

CHAPTER 25

LIFE IS ABOUT CREATING YOURSELF

"*Life isn't about finding yourself. Life is about creating yourself.*" – **George Bernard Shaw**, (1856–1950 Irish playwright and Nobel Prize winner in Literature)

"*Remember, happiness doesn't depend upon who you are or what you have, it depends solely upon what you think.*" – **Dale Carnegie**, (1888–1955 American author and speaker)

"*No one is in control of your happiness but you. Therefore, you have the power to change anything about yourself or your life that you want to change.*" – **Barbara De Angelis**, (relationship guru and best selling author)

Did you know that your brain can hold only ONE bit of information in any given moment? This is a very important fact.

Why?

Because if you are focusing on something negative and unpleasant, everything positive that you are experiencing in your life is lost at that moment. And there is always something positive in your life if you only look for it. It is YOUR choice!

Action Steps

Next time you catch yourself thinking a negative thought or picturing a negative outcome...STOP! Erase that negative thought and that picture and replace it with what you WANT to happen. Here are some ways to do it:

1. Mentally delete the unwanted information as if it was on a computer screen. See the blank page and design a positive picture for the desired outcome.
2. Imagine the image is on a regular piece of paper. See yourself as you tear that paper into tiny little pieces. Then take out a new paper and paint a new image.
3. Another approach is to rewind the "old message" or the memory of what has happened and record a new more positive version over it.

Eventually you will discover your own personal way of replacing negative thoughts and visions with positive ones that work best for you.

CHAPTER 26

HOW SUCCESSFUL PEOPLE DEAL WITH FAILURE

What is failure? Is failure the opposite of success? Do you believe in failure? How do you feel about failure? How we feel about failure is greatly related to how successful we become.

I personally do not believe in failure. I believe that the only way I can fail is by giving up! It is ok for me to make mistakes and to fall down sometimes. In fact, it indicates to me that I try and take risks. It is when I choose to stay down that I would consider myself a failure.

I came to this empowering belief because I learnt from people I admire. Today I want you to think about failure and analyze how other people we hold in our esteem and consider to be successful, have dealt or still deal with failure:

"I feel that the most important requirement in success is learning to overcome failure. You must learn to tolerate it, but never accept it." - **Reggie Jackson**, (member of the Baseball Hall of Fame)

"A man's life is interesting primarily when he had failed – for it's a sign that he tried to surpass himself." - **Georges Clemenceau**, (1841–1929 French statesman, physician and journalist)

"A man can get discouraged many times but he is not a failure until he begins to blame somebody else and stops trying." - **John Burroughs**, (1837–1921 American naturalist and essayist)

"If you don't fail now and again, it's a sign you're playing it safe." - **Woody Allen**, (Academy Award-winning American film director and actor)

"My great concern is not whether you have failed, but whether you are content with your failure." - **Abraham Lincoln**, (1809–1865 16th President of the United States)

"The only man who never makes mistakes is the man who never does anything." - **Theodore Roosevelt**, (1858–1919 26th President of the United States)

"The men who try to do something and fail are infinitely better than those who try to do nothing and succeed." - **Martin Lloyd Jones**, (1899–1981 Welsh Theologian)

"He's no failure. He's not dead yet." - **William Lloyd George**

Action Steps

1. If you find yourself feeling like a failure, go back to this page and read the quotes again.
2. Realise that although you might not always control what happens to you, you are always in control of how you REACT to it.
3. Create your own empowering belief about 'failure' then use it for yourself and share it with others.

CHAPTER 27

WHAT DOES IT TAKE TO BE ATTRACTIVE?

All around me I see people rushing to buy beautiful clothes, going to the hairdressers, having their manicures and pedicures done, facials and make-up. All in the desire to look attractive for that special party or date. I also notice that very few people focus on the most important aspect of beauty – the beauty within!

How many times have you seen a person with a strikingly beautiful face and body, but who is not 'attractive' at all (often after you start speaking to them)? And other times you will meet someone who is not "really beautiful" yet you feel totally attracted to that person. He or she might not even "be your type" but you still find them very attractive. Why?

Being attractive comes from having that magnetic power that pulls people towards you. A power that inspires them to talk to you and find out more about who you are-a power that makes them want to be like you!

Action Steps

1. Feel good about how you look. It is good and very healthy to want to look beautiful and spend time working on it. When you look good, you feel good and that adds to your inner attraction.
2. Feel good about who you are as a person. Work on your self-esteem. Be confident in your own skin. CONFIDENCE is the greatest attraction of all! To do that, only think good things of yourself and do affirmations such as "I like myself!" "I am very attractive" "I allow myself to be liked and admired for who I am".
3. If you want others to like you, like THEM first. Be careful of what you are thinking. What you think and feel is communicated to others subliminally. Compliment someone that you like in your mind and see how attractive they will find YOU!
4. SMILE! It is easy to do and easy not to, but a smile adds tremendously to your attractiveness.
5. Finally, focus on who you are and not just what you look like. People fall in love with the essence of you – your energy, the sparkle in your eyes, your passion for living, your unconditional love, everything that makes you unique and special…people fall in love with your beautiful soul!

CHAPTER 28

HOW MUCH DO YOU LOVE YOURSELF?

Let's talk about LOVE. More specifically, I would like to focus on self-love. Why?
Because you cannot give more than you have – in order to give and receive love, you have to first love yourself. According to the last statement, would you say it is logical to conclude that we are capable of giving love in direct proportion to how much we actually love and like ourselves?

Moreover, what if we allowed others to love and like us in direct proportion to how much we love and like ourselves?

Action Steps

1. Think about how your past and current relationships have been affected due to the information above. If you have had negative experiences with love and feel you might have sabotaged yourself in the past, maybe it is because you feel you do not deserve to be loved.
2. Decide today (or as soon as you are ready) that you deserve to be loved FOR WHO YOU ARE! You do not need to prove your worth to anyone. Think about a newborn baby who is loved unconditionally the minute he or she is born.
3. Forgive yourself for past mistakes and accept yourself with all your wonderful imperfections as well as your unique talents. Love yourself for who you are and the world will love you in return!

CHAPTER 29

THE SECRET TO A GREAT LIFE

"I never ran 1000 miles. I could never have done that. I ran one mile 1000 times." – **Stu Mittleman**, (World Record Holder for Ultra-Distance Running)

"And in the end, it's not the years in your life that count. It's the life in your years." – **Abraham Lincoln**

What is the secret to having a great life? Well, if you had to divide life into measurable bits, you could start with years. So to have a great life you would have to start by first having a set of great years one after another.

You could then divide years into months. Therefore, to have a great year you would focus on having a great 12 months (one month at a time). To have a great month, you would need to have 4 great weeks. To have a great week, all you have to do is just focus on having 7 great days.

My conclusion? To have a great life, ultimately you have to have a GREAT DAY! One day at a time. This simple conclusion has changed my life! I value every day to the fullest and do my best to make it as successful, productive and happy as I can. Every single day represents life to me, because that is what life is made of – days, hours, minutes, seconds, moments…

If you look at each moment as a precious part of YOUR life and live it to the fullest, you will be very happy and fulfilled indeed!

Action Steps

Value and make the best of each day, each hour and each minute of your life. Be conscious that once it is gone, it is gone forever...

PART 5

ARE YOU A NATURAL LEADER

CHAPTER 30

ARE YOU A NATURAL LEADER?

"*The greatest privilege of leadership is the chance to elevate lives*" – **Robin Sharma**, (best-selling author of The Monk Who Sold His Ferrari)

Are great leaders born or made? What does it mean to be a great leader?

In a society of hierarchies it is often assumed that CEOs, company owners, and other people in positions of power are the leaders. In fact, position has nothing to do with it! One can be in charge of hundreds of people and not be a leader at all. At the same time, someone without a management or leadership position can be a great leader. Are you?

Leadership is not about position. Leadership is about inspiring, motivating and influencing others to follow your cause. It's about passion. It's about action. It's about having great dreams and then doing all it takes to manifest them.

Leadership is not about managing people but about developing them. A great leader is someone who allows and encourages others to develop their highest potential, express their individuality and honor their lives.

Action Steps

Great leadership begins within YOU. You cannot be a great leader of other lives before you can effectively lead your own. Ask yourself:

- What am I passionate about?
- Do I have a compelling vision that inspires and motivates me?
- Do I have the discipline that helps make the right choices and take action steps that bring me closer to my vision?
- Do I understand the values that drive me and live by them?
- Do I honor my own life and am I true to myself?
- Do I allow myself to express my highest potential and believe that I am here to make a difference?

Remember, you are unique and have something to offer to this world that no one else has. Have the courage to unleash your genius and be the light that others want to follow.

CHAPTER 31

THE POWER OF A TEAM AND CO-OPERATION

Most of my work is focused on researching and understanding what makes some people more successful than others – understanding the mindset behind success. One thing successful people recognize and maximize is the power of a good team. Let me share the following story with you that I believe will demonstrate my point effectively:

A man died and fortunately for him, he went to heaven, where he met God. The Almighty welcomed him to heaven but then asked him: "Do you have any last wish, my son, before you spend the rest of eternity in heaven?" "Yes," said the man. "I would like to know what Hell is like so I can more thoroughly appreciate my good fortune." God replied: "Fine," snapped his fingers and instantly they were in Hell.

Before them was an impossibly long table piled high with the most wonderful delicacies that anyone's heart could desire and on both sides of the table were perched millions of unhappy people starving to death. The man turned to God and asked: "Why are all these people starving?" God replied: "Everyone must eat from the table with 10 foot long chopsticks." "That's terribly harsh," the man said compassionately. God snapped his fingers again, and suddenly they were back in heaven.

However, on entering heaven, the man was surprised to see an almost identical scene! A huge long table piled eye with food and again millions of people either side, except this time, everyone seemed happy and well-fed. He turned to God and asked:

"What do the people eat with here? Can they use knife and forks?" "No, my son," said God. "Everyone here also eats with 10 foot long chopsticks." The man was confused. "I don't understand. How are they managing to feed themselves?" God replied: "In heaven, we feed each other."

On earth, as in heaven, when we take care of each other's needs and work together, no one goes 'unfed.'

Action Steps

1. Look at your goals (personal and professional) and analyze how you can create leverage by involving other people. For example, when I was a stay-at-home mom and wanted to start my own business, I realized that I would need help to achieve it. Initially, a part of my 'team' became a cleaner and my parents-in-law. As my business and my family grew, so did my team. Because I have a team, I can organize my time in a way that creates a balanced and fulfilling life.
2. Do not be afraid to ask for help or assistance. In life, we should not only be able to give unconditionally but to also accept unconditionally.
3. Finally, remember that the best way to achieve what you want, is to help someone else achieve it.

CHAPTER 32

USING WORDS WITH GOOD PURPOSE

Did you know that you can positively transform your environment just by changing the words that you use? How you use your words is critical because whatever you say eventually comes back to you like a boomerang. How the people around you use their words also affects you. The concept of Neuro-Linguistic Programming is based on this fact.

If you are a leader in your company (or in your home) you can use this practical example to ensure a positive environment around you. I found this example in one of my favourite books "The One Minute Millionaire" by **Mark Victor Hansen** and **Robert G. Allen.**

Marshall Thurber, a partner in one of the most successful real estate companies in San Francisco, told of a powerful experiment he conducted with his office staff. "There was one discipline that immediately transformed my entire organization. It developed from one of our weekly Monday morning meetings with the entire company. At that meeting I read a page from a book detailing the life of **Rolling Thunder**, an American Indian medicine man."

These are **Rolling Thunder's** words:

"People have to be responsible for their thoughts, so they have to learn to control them. It may not be easy, but it can be done. First of all, if we don't want to think certain things we don't say them. We don't have to eat everything we see, and we don't have to say everything we think. So we begin by watching our words and speaking with good purpose only."

Upon reading this quote, everyone in Thurber's company agreed to only speak with good purpose. That is, *"If it doesn't serve, don't say."* According to their rules, if anyone was observed not following the policy of speaking with good purpose, he or she agreed to donate $2 to a bowl in the office. At the end of the month the money in the bowl was given to charity.

This simple act of putting $2 into a bowl was a transforming experience for this entire office. According to Thurber, nothing he has done before or since had such a powerful impact on a group of people.

Action Steps

1. Choose your words carefully. Only speak with good purpose. If it doesn't serve, don't say it. If you catch yourself speaking words that don't serve, pay your penalty into a bowl.
2. Encourage others around you to do the same. Then watch the results in your own life, your home, or your office.

CHAPTER 33

PERSONAL SATISFACTION AT WORK

"*We can change our lives. We can do, have, and be exactly what we wish.*"
– **Anthony Robbins**

Do you know what the most frequently mentioned measure of success in work-life is? According to **Kouzes** and **Posner**, authors of *The Leadership Challenge*, as surprising as it might sound, it is "personal satisfaction for doing a good job." This reason is cited 3–4 times as often as "getting ahead" or "making a good living."

Personal satisfaction for doing a good job comes from understanding your purpose and values and aligning them with the company you work for. It also comes from being recognized and valued for what you do and who you are.

When we feel that our efforts go unrewarded and unrecognized, it af-fects our self-esteem and overall performance. At the same time, being dependent on other people for getting recognition can create frustration, dissatisfaction and even depression.

But, as the Irish Author & Playwright **George Bernard Shaw** points out: "*People are always blaming their circumstances for what they are. I don't believe in circumstances. The people who get on in this world are the people who get up and look for the circumstances they want, and, if they can't find them, make them.*"

Action Steps

1. Clarify your own purpose and values and make sure your environment supports them.
2. Value yourself and what you do. And remember, the best way to get what you want is to give it first. So give recognition to people around you and make them feel valued when opportunity comes.
3. Finally, decide who is in control – you or your circumstances. If you can't find the circumstances that you want, make them! This is the winning attitude of all successful people.

CHAPTER 34

HELPING IS NOT ALWAYS GOOD

"*A good deed in the wrong place is like an evil deed.*" – **Marcus Tullius Cicero**, (106-43 BC Roman statesman and writer)

It is important to find a balance in ALL that we do, including helping others. Here is an example of what I mean:

In a Boy Scout meeting, two friends are reporting their good deeds for the week to their scoutmaster.

The first one gets up and reports that he's helped an old lady across the street. Then the next gets up and reports that he's helped the same old lady across the street. The scoutmaster looks puzzled and asks them:

"*Why did it take both of you to help the same old lady across the street?*"

In unison they reply: "*That's because she didn't want to go.*"

Action Steps

1. You probably know from your own experience that people will not be receptive to help or advice if they are not ready for it or don't really want it. So, before volunteering your help or advice to someone, ask yourself:
    - What is my intention?
    - Am I really seeing the problem from that person's point of view?
    - Does this person want to be helped?
    - What is the best way to approach this person?
    - When is the best time to do it?
2. What I find works best is first ASKING the person if they want your opinion or advice. Most of the time, people reply "yes" and then it is 'safe' to proceed, ensuring that your message will come across the way you want it. And if the response is a "no" then let it go and try again another time. As an old saying goes: "Never try to teach a pig to sing. It wastes your time and it annoys the pig."

CHAPTER 35

WHAT IS YOUR GREATNESS?

"*Treat people as if they were what they ought to be and you help them to become what they are capable of being.*" – **Johann Wolfgang von Goethe**, (1749–1832 German philosopher, poet and writer)

The importance of valuing your own and other people's differences is demonstrated so well in this parable:

"The Animal School" by **Dr. R.H. Reeves**

Once upon a time, the animals decided they must do something heroic to meet the problems of a 'New World,' so they organized a school. They adopted an activity curriculum consisting of running, climbing, swimming and flying. To make it easier to administer, all animals took all the subjects.

The duck was excellent in swimming, better in fact than his instructor, and made excellent grades in flying, but he was very poor in running. Since he was low in running he had to stay after school and also drop swimming to practice running. This was kept up until his web feet were badly worn and he was only average in swimming. But average was acceptable in school, so nobody worried about that, except the duck.

The rabbit started at the top of the class in running, but had a nervous breakdown because he had so much to make up in swimming. The squirrel was excellent in climbing until he developed frustrations in the flying class where his teacher made him start from the ground up instead of from the tree-top down. He also developed charley horses from overexertion and he got a C in climbing and a D in running.

The eagle was a problem child and had to be disciplined severely. In climbing class he beat all the others to the top of the tree, but insisted on using his own way of getting there. At the end of the year, an abnormal eel that could swim exceedingly well and could also run, climb and fly a little had the highest average and was valedictorian.

Action Steps

1. Do not settle for an average; do not settle for second best. Discover what you are already good at and what you are passionate about and then dedicate all your energy and time to developing your strengths – to achieving your greatness!
2. Be an effective leader and focus on people's strengths and what they are already good at. Then inspire them to become great at it!

CHAPTER 36

ARE YOU BUSY BEING BUSY?

"*Don't just do something, sit there! Sit there long enough each morning to decide what is really important during the day ahead.*" – **Sir Richard Eyre**, (English film and theatre director)

Do you find yourself busy attending to lots of urgent and important matters but feeling that you are not really going anywhere? Or that you are moving rapidly but not quite sure where? Are you so busy catching up, that life just seems to be passing by without you really having time to reflect on it and to enjoy it fully?

Unfortunately, this is the usual scenario of busy executives, parents, business owners and anyone who is doing their best to live up to "life's expectations". Yet, if you wait until you just make a bit more money, or until the children are older, or until business picks up, or until you retire, or until… fill the blank, then IT MIGHT NEVER HAPPEN!

When you wait for something to happen in order to do what you want, you voluntarily give up your control about your life and rely on circumstances. Stop waiting till the 'right time' and MAKE that time now.

Action Steps

1. Take out your appointment book and schedule a daily meeting with your most important client – yourself. Make it an uninterrupted time to just sit and think… just relax and reflect, contemplate, feel… just BE.
2. If you are not used to just being because you are always doing something, be patient with yourself. It will take time to be able to just sit and do nothing, but it might become the most productive time of your day!

PART 6

TIME MANAGEMENT & DECISION MAKING

CHAPTER 37

EFFECTIVE DECISION MAKING

"*To win or lose, to love or hate, to try or quit, to risk or withdraw, to accelerate or hesitate. to dream or stagnate, to open or close, to succeed or fail, to live or die. Everyone of these starts with a CHOICE.*" – **Snowden McFall**, (author, trainer and personal coach)

"*Regret for the things we did can be tempered by time; it is regret for the things we did not do that is inconsolable.*" – **Sydney J. Harris**, (1917–1986 American journalist)

There is nothing in this world that you do in the course of your lifetime that can bring you greater success than the ability to make better choices and decisions. The ability to make choices is one of the most valuable gifts we, as humans, possess. Since life ultimately consists of making choices, the quality of your life depends on the quality of choices that you make!

If you are not happy with any aspect of your life, it is up to you to change it. How? By making decisions that carry with them the consequences YOU desire.

In 1970, sociologist **Dr. Edward Banfield** of Harvard University wrote a book entitled The Unheavenly City. He described one of the most profound studies on success and priority setting ever conducted. What he discovered was that the major reason for success in life was a particular attitude of mind.

Banfield called this attitude "long time perspective." He said that men and women who were the most successful in life and the most likely to progress economically were those who took the future into consideration with every decision they made in the present.

Being responsible for your future is an empowering belief! So use your personal power, make sound decisions and start creating the life you want to have.

Effective Decision Making

Action Steps

1. The formula for effective decision making is very simple – every decision that moves you TOWARDS your goals and dreams is an effective decision and every decision that moves you AWAY from your goals, wastes your valuable time.
2. Next time you find yourself not knowing what decision to make, use this great question for an effective solution: 'Does this decision move me closer to the achievement of my goals and my vision or away from them?' This simple process of stopping and asking this question creates a decision making habit that will help you reach your goals faster. It will eliminate many frustrations and will improve your overall quality of life.

CHAPTER 38

HOW MUCH DO YOU RELY ON LOGIC?

Do you make your decisions using mainly your logic, or your intuition? The following parable, called *"The Expert,"* was shared with me by **Dr. Bill Gould**, the founder of *Transformation Thinking* and a good friend of mine:

Once there was a group of people that were in the habit of cutting off those heads that contained opinions different from the ones they were pushing at the time. One day they brought along a cart to where they had the guillotine set up. In this cart were three people: a consumer, a businessman, and an "expert."

First, the consumer was put on the guillotine. The lever was pulled and down came the blade and jammed one inch above the consumer's head. The crowd was unanimous, "This was an act of God!" So they let the consumer free, and being a good consumer, he went away muttering about the poor quality of the equipment.

Next, they put the businessman on the guillotine. The lever was pulled and down came the blade and, once again, it jammed one inch above the businessman's head. Again the crowd cried out, "Set him free!" and they did. Being a good businessman, he went away with ideas for starting a guillotine repair service.

Finally, they were about to get the "expert," but he leapt up onto the platform and with a gleam in his eye, he said, "You know, if you would just tighten that screw there and this one here, you will find that the machine will work perfectly"...and of course, it did!

Logically, the "expert" was correct, but perhaps there was something inadequate about his PERCEPTION of the situation.

As Dr. Bill Gould points out, logic may often lead us to the correct conclusion, but it is one's overall perception of events that provide the wisdom necessary to arrive at better decisions as to how and when to apply that logic.

Action Steps

1. Though thinking your decision through logically is good, relying solely on logic can lead to some 'painful' experiences. Always listen to your intuition, to your gut, to your 6th sense... Consciously we might not know all the answers (nor should we strive to have them) but if you are able to connect to the higher power, you will know what is the right direction for you to take.
2. Finally, remember that ANY decision is better than indecision.

CHAPTER 39

ARE THERE BAD DECISIONS?

Do you believe that there are bad decisions? If yes, what would be a bad decision for you?

My philosophy is that there are no good or bad decisions – there are only consequences. To avoid the consequences you do not desire to experience, stop and analyze how your decision will affect you in the future.

A decision is like a pebble you toss into a quiet pond. The ripples that emanate from the center and travel outwards in 360 degrees are the effects of that decision. As the ripples flow outwards, they touch everything in their path.

It is the same with your choices and decisions. They affect everyone around us directly or indirectly. What happens when the ripples reach the far shore? They immediately reverse their direction and return to the source. There are many expressions we use to express this concept like *'What goes around comes around,'* or *'You reap what you sow'* or *'You get back what you put in.'*

Once the pebble has left your hand, it is too late to stop the ripples and they DO always return to the source. That is why it is so important to consider the consequences and ramifications of what we say and do BEFORE we commit ourselves by our behavior.

And another question to think about… If the ripples that your decision (your pebble) has created touch a leaf on which a frog is sitting and the frog falls into the water, creating more ripples, who is responsible for those ripples – you or the frog?

The answer is, BOTH.

Action Steps

1. Yes, your decisions affect you and those around you but it is important not to be afraid to make your decisions. You see, if you want to 'play safe' and not do something just in case there will be unpleasant consequences, keep in mind what **Dr. Bill Gould** said: "There are not only ripples for what we do. There are also ripples for what we should or could have done and didn't."
2. Make brave and effective decisions, take smart risks and enjoy the journey to your success. In fact, my definition of success IS this journey!

CHAPTER 40

THE CURRENCY OF TODAY

Effective time management is an integral part to any success. In fact, it is considered the currency of today. Let me share with you a simple but very important tip to getting more done in a shorter time.

Do you find yourself spending a lot of time thinking about what you are not doing and beating yourself up for not doing it? Do you often look forward to doing something particular that you consider fun, recreational, or just more productive, while you are engaged in another activity?

Most of us do. Unfortunately, these kinds of mental activities prevent you from being present with the job at hand and waste a lot of your precious time.

The best way to create a clear focus and get your tasks done much more easily and effectively is to follow this rule:

Do what you do when you're doing it, and don't do what you're not doing when you're not doing it.

Please read the previous sentence again and let it sink in. Being 'in the moment' is not relevant to just the good times, in fact the more focused you are on the present task at any particular moment, the more productive you are and the less stress you experience in your life.

Action Steps

- If you are eating, take time to enjoy your food.
- If you are with your children, your spouse or your friend, just be fully with them, do not worry about what needs to be done and when.
- If you are working on a project at work, decide exactly how much and by when you want to achieve in regards to that project and do not do anything else until you get there.
- The same applies to everything else, of course.

CHAPTER 41

CREATING A BALANCED LIFE

Are you functioning at your maximum standard of living? Do you want to get more from life? Do you want to give more back?

Many people are so passionate about what they are doing, so focused on their commitment and so involved in their work that one part of their lives is a model of excellence, while the rest is in ruin.

Many people understand the value of BALANCE and have probably made numerous attempts to achieve it, with good intentions to exercise more, or take a little time off, or to reconnect with friends, but then find that weeks or months pass without any action.

At today's pace of life, with so many responsibilities, attractive options, demands, and distractions, balance may feel like an impossible dream. Yet, nobody likes to feel 'out of balance' and living a balanced life is integral to functioning at your highest standard of living.

Creating a Balanced Life | **93**

Action Steps

1. If you are working hard to make money and pay the bills, postponing everything else in your life 'till the better times,' you are making a big mistake. To create more balance in your life, first realize that getting proper rest, looking after your physical, mental and emotional well-being as well as spending quality time with your loved ones, actually adds to your productivity. Once you create this transformational belief, focus on 'sharing yourself' equally in all areas of your life.
2. Create weekly schedules. For example, come up with a day of the week and the time that you will dedicate to your most important client – yourself. Do the same for your loved ones, for your career, for your health, for your goals. Remember, if you do not MAKE the time to do the things you want to do, it might never happen.

CHAPTER 42

THE VALUE OF AN HOUR

"*Days are expensive. When you spend a day you have one less day to spend. So make sure you spend each one wisely.*" – **Jim Rohn**, (motivational speaker)

Do you feel there is not enough time to do what you want to do? For example, you might want to learn a foreign language; get a degree from the University, exercise more, have more time to be alone and reflect on life, or spend more quality time with your loved ones...

Before I share with you how to do all those things you are currently lacking the time to do, let me ask you: *How good can you get at something if you did it all day, every day for just over 2 months?*

Well, if you invest just one hour each day in your chosen activity, you will accumulate nine 40-hour weeks over the course of just one year! (365 days, times one hour each is nine 40-hour weeks).

In fact, with only an hour a day, over the course of five years, you would have invested the equivalent of 1,825 hours of focus on whatever you desire to accomplish in your life! Imagine for a minute, how good you can become at anything that you did one hour a day for the next year!

How fit could you get? How much more love could you get and give? How much more money could you earn? Let me suggest that one hour is a small price to pay in comparison to the pay off. Just one hour a day may be the razor's edge you need to really get the results you want in your life.

Action Steps

1. Adopt an hour a day for yourself! If you feel that your schedule is too busy to find that hour, re-evaluate your values and priorities and remind yourself that you are in control of your life and your time.
2. Pick one area of your life that you want to improve and commit to focus on it for an hour a day for the next 90 days. I assure you that the results you achieve will be well worth the decision!

And remember...you can't take out of life more than you put in.

CHAPTER 43

THE SLOWER YOU GO, THE FASTER YOU WILL GET THERE

Are you so busy focusing on what you want – on the rewards after all that hard work you put in – that you miss out on the journey? Are you going so fast that there is no time to stop and ask yourself WHY? If your answer is 'yes' then according to this fable, you are actually being counter productive. Because the faster you go, the longer it will take you to get there:

Once a young student traveled many miles to find a famous spiritual master. When he finally met this man, he told him that his main goal in life was to be the wisest man in the land. This is why he needed the best teacher. Seeing the young boy's enthusiasm, the master agreed to share his knowledge with him and took him under his wing.

"How long will it take before I find enlightenment?" the boy immediately asked.

"At least five years," replied the master. "That is too long," said the boy. "I cannot wait five years! What if I study twice as hard as the rest of your students?"

"Ten years," came the response.

"Ten years! Well, then, how about if I studied day and night, with every ounce of my mental concentration? Then how long would it take for me to become the wise man that I've always dreamed of becoming?"

"Fifteen years," replied the master.

The boy grew very frustrated. "How come every time I tell you I will work harder to reach my goal, you tell me it will take longer?"

"The answer is clear," said the teacher: "With one eye focused on the reward, there is only one eye left to focus on your purpose."

It is important to stop and reflect on WHY you want what you want. What is the purpose of your journey?

When you focus your energies on the worthy purpose rather then the end result, you will get to your destination much faster; you will achieve greater fulfillment and you will live your life much more fully!

Action Steps

Time is your most valuable commodity, be careful how you spend it and be clear what you are working so hard to achieve. If the outcome is worth it, then relax and enjoy the journey!

CHAPTER 44

ARE YOU LIVING FOR THE FUTURE?

"*Life is what happens when we are busy making plans*" – **John Lennon**, (1940–1980 British singer, song-writer and founder of the legendary Beatles band)

Most, if not all, of the great leaders and achievers take plenty of time to relax and reflect. Take time to enjoy life. Do YOU?

So often we postpone what we really want to do for later. We say to ourselves, "When I have more money... when I have more time... when the kids grow up... when I am not so busy... when I retire..." So often we are living for the future and yet... the next day is promised to no one!

I knew a man who worked hard and had great plans to travel, buy a new house, even get married after he retired. When he finally retired, he did buy a new house and was found dead in it just 3 weeks later, alone and without a chance to do all those things that he had planned for when the 'time was right'...

Yes, it is important to think and plan for the future, but it is also just as important to realize that life is happening NOW. So, take time to enjoy life, time off with your loved ones, time off for yourself – time to do NOTHING, to just BE.

Action Steps

1. Realize right now that YOU are in control of your life – not your bank statements, not the people around you, not your circumstances. Every decision that you make every choice that you have is YOURS.
2. CHOOSE to do something really good for yourself. Take your yearly planner and schedule in your next vacation. Whether you think you can do it or not, just schedule it in, make plans for it and see how it will work out for you.
3. Make an appointment with yourself. Decide on an hour each day that is just for you to do what feeds your soul. If you can take more time, great. If you can't find an hour, start with 20 minutes and then add to it.

Remember, it's the space BETWEEN the notes that makes the music.

PART 7

THE BEST SOURCE OF WEALTH

CHAPTER 45

PRODUCE THE RESULTS YOU ARE LOOKING FOR

"*The definition of insanity is doing the same thing over and over again and expecting different results.*" – **Albert Einstein**, (1879–1955 one of the greatest physicists of all time)

Did you know that statistically over 90% of people give up on their goals and New Year resolutions within 3 weeks of setting them?! Did you ever wonder WHY so many people with great intentions to do what is right, who set goals and new year resolutions and then, one year later, realize that what they set for themselves they haven't accomplished?

Then, with new enthusiasm they do it again just to get disappointed later. It becomes a vicious circle and unfortunately many people give up making goals in life. They would rather not have goals than feel bad for not following them through.

Unfortunately, when this happens people tend to think that something is wrong with THEM! Their self-esteem goes down and low self-esteem is one of the major reasons for not succeeding. But here is some good news – not following through with goals has NOTHING to do with who you are…

If you have a great desire to succeed but are not getting what you want, then you are simply missing the right tools to do it. For a change to take place in your life and for your goals to come true you do not need much! Most of what you need you already have!

At the same time, it is important to remember that whatever got you to where you are today is not enough to keep you there. For you to move forward and achieve your goals, it is important that you constantly improve yourself – that you constantly acquire new skills, stay open to new ideas and integrate your new knowledge with what you already know.

It is these NEW CONNECTIONS that will help you produce the results you are looking for.

Action Steps

1. Help yourself grow and develop in the direction you want to go. Decide how much time and money you will dedicate this year on personal development.
2. Decide what it is you really want to learn and then find appropriate courses and/or teachers for it.
3. Do it today! If you expect different results, then do things differently, be pro-active and be persistent!

CHAPTER 46

WHAT DID YOU MISS OUT ON TODAY?

If a man empties his purse into his head, no man can take it away from him. An investment in knowledge always pays the best interest. - **Benjamin Franklin** (1706–1790, one of the best-known Founding Fathers of the United States)

Develop a passion for learning. If you do, you will never cease to grow. - **Anthony J. D'Angelo** (American Writer)

One of the things successful people have in common is their passion for learning.

T.H. White in his book, *The Once and Future King*, expresses the power of learning very eloquently. "The best thing for being sad," replied Merlin, beginning to puff and blow, "is to learn something. That's the only thing that never fails. You may grow old and trembling in your anatomies, you may lie awake at night listening to the disorder of your veins, you may miss your only love, you may see the world about you devastated by evil lunatics, or know your honour trampled in the sewers of baser minds. There is only one thing for it then – to learn. Learn why the world wags and what wags it. That is the only thing which the mind can never exhaust, never alienate, never be tortured by, never fear or distrust, and never dream of regretting. Learning is the only thing for you. Look what a lot of things there are to learn."

Henry Ford, a business magnate who founded the Ford Motors Company said, "If money is your hope for independence, you will never have it. The only real security that a man will have in this world is a reserve of knowledge, experience, and ability."

Clint Eastwood, a Hollywood icon, once remarked: "I'd like to be a bigger and more knowledgeable person ten years from now than I am today. I think that, for all of us, as we grow older, we must discipline ourselves to continue expanding, broadening, learning, keeping our minds active and open."

And I will end this chapter with the wise words of Mahatma Gandhi, who helped to free India from the British rule,

"Live as if you were to die tomorrow. Learn as if you were to live forever."

Action Steps

1. Make time for reading about topics that interest and inspire you. As Jim Rohn points out: "The only thing worse than not reading a book in the last ninety days is not reading a book in the last ninety days and thinking that it doesn't matter."
2. At least twice a year, attend a workshop or a seminar. Not only will you pick up new ideas and increase your knowledge base, but also you will meet like-minded people and often make long-lasting friendships.
3. Cultivate the learning habit, and inspire others to do the same. Before you go to bed, ask yourself, "What did I learn today?" Write the answer down in your journal, and review it regularly. It is very empowering!

CHAPTER 47

THE POWER OF QUESTIONS

"*The quality of our lives is closely related to the quality of our questions.*" – **Michael Angier**, (speaker and founder of Success Networks)

- What is wrong with me?
- Why does this always happen to me?
- Why don't I like myself?
- I am such an idiot! Why did I have to do that?

Do you find you asking yourself these kinds of questions in your day-to-day life? Many people do. It seems easier or even more honorable in some way to beat yourself up rather than praise yourself for a job well done. Why?

Though it might be interesting for you to analyze why that is happening, it is more important to understand that whatever you ask your brain, it WILL find you an answer! It is just the way your brain operates. Understanding that, you can use it to your advantage rather than against you.

If you ask your brain "What is wrong with me?" Your brain will reply with a lot of very good answers, even if they are not real, just because you asked!

What if instead you asked yourself questions such as:

- What is good about me?
- What did I do to deserve all these wonderful things in my life?
- What can I do or think to like myself more?
- I am only human and I made a mistake. How can I learn from it?

Whatever you ask, you will get an answer. Whatever you focus on becomes your reality. Use the power of questions to get the answers you REALLY want!

Action Steps

1. Come up with 5 empowering and motivational questions to prepare yourself each morning for the successful day ahead of you.
2. Change your questions every 10 days, depending on what answers you want to know at this time in your life. Some example questions are:
    - Who or what in my life makes me feel the happiest?
    - How can I make enough money within 6 months to buy the car that I want?
    - How can I be a better leader today?
    - What can I do today to make my loved ones happy?

CHAPTER 48

ASK AND YOU WILL RECEIVE

"*Quality questions create a quality life. Successful people ask better questions and as a result, they get better answers.*" – **Anthony Robbins**

Continuing on the topic of questions, let me share with you a great example of how one successful person learnt to use questions effectively in his life. This example comes from a book called "The 11th Element" by **Robert Scheinfeld**

Bill Harris, owner of the *Centerpoint Research Institute* in Oregon whose company sells a very powerful meditation program, wrote to Mr. Scheinfeld explaining how asking the right questions helped him build his successful business:

> One of the most amazing things I've found in my success has been the ability to tap into the answer for any question I need answered, just by continually asking it. For this reason, I find I can undertake and successfully accomplish any project or endeavor without knowing in advance how I'm going to bring it to the finish line.
>
> I just ask *"How am I going to get more people to buy my product, or how can I raise the money I need for this, or how can I get more visitors to my web site to actually buy my product,"* or any other question. As far as I'm concerned, the more difficult and outrageous the question, the more fun the challenge is!
>
> I find that focusing on the question always brings the answer to me. Either it pops into my head, or a book pops off the shelf at the bookstore, or I meet someone who has the answer, or I overhear a snatch of a conversation in a crowd from someone who knows the answer, or it comes to me in some other way – often one I would never have anticipated. What I need to know appears.
>
> But I have come to rely on this phenomenon to such a degree that I never worry any more about how I will find an answer.
>
> No matter how tough the problem, I just know that if I continually focus on the question, the answer will come. Some unseen force always sends the answer if you put out the call and just keep asking.
>
> Using this method, I've been able to build my business from $12,000 in annual sales in 1990 to over $4.6 million in 2001. My goal is $35 million annually and I have no doubt I will reach it.

Action Steps

How can YOU use the power of questions to produce desired results in YOUR life?

Simply make quality questions one of your empowering habits and as a result, enjoy a better quality of life!

CHAPTER 49

EXCELLENCE IS NOT AN ACT, BUT A HABIT

"We are what we repeatedly do. Excellence then, is not an act, but a habit." – **Aristotle**, (384–382 BCE Greek philosopher)

Most people do not realize what kind of power our habits hold over us! Why? Because habits are often unconscious, yet consistent patterns that constantly express our character and the results we produce (or do not produce) on a regular basis. As the maxim goes, "Sow a thought, reap an action; sow an action, reap a habit; sow a habit, reap a character; sow a character, reap a destiny!"

Stephen R. Covey, the author of the well-known best-seller *"The Seven Habits of Highly Effective People"* defines a habit as the intersection of knowledge, skill and desire. In Covey's definition, knowledge is the WHAT to do and the why. Skill is the HOW to do. Desire and motivation are the WANT to do.

In order to make something a habit in your life, all three ingredients must be present.

Action Steps

No matter what you want in your life, chances are, someone out there already has it. Find these people. Study and understand their habits and their belief system. In essence, to become a millionaire, study and adopt the millionaire's money habits; to be fit and healthy, study and adopt the habits of those who are fit and healthy.

Start with these 3 simple actions every day for the next 30 days:

1. Get absolutely clear on the outcome you want to achieve. Write it down.
2. Replay in your head having already achieved your outcome. See all the benefits. Imagine what you would be doing, who would be impacted, what conversations you would be having and how you would feel. Spend 5 to 10 minutes fully in this experience every morning as you wake up and again just before bed.
3. Re-affirm the following affirmation as many times as you can daily: "I now have everything I need to accomplish all of my business and personal goals. Happiness is my birthright and I accept it NOW."

CHAPTER 50

THE BEST SOURCE OF WEALTH

"Formal education will make you a living, self-education will make you a fortune." – **Jim Rohn**

What is the best source of wealth? In the Information Age, wealth is not contained in raw material, land, factories, or any other material assets, as it used to be throughout history, but more in our ability to learn, re-learn, and acquire knowledge faster and in a more efficient way than others. Today, the best source of wealth is in-between our ears – OUR MIND POWER.

People who do not update their skills and knowledge on an ongoing basis are, unfortunately, either getting fired at work, afraid that they will get fired or living in fear of uncertainty blaming their circumstances for what is happening in their lives.

The good news is that you can achieve any goal, solve almost any problem, and overcome almost any obstacle by acquiring the necessary knowledge and skills required for that particular situation. In fact, constantly looking for opportunities to learn and to grow is a major part of the mindset of people who are successful and who get ahead in this competitive world.

Why is it then that so many adults deny themselves what should be one of the most enriching parts of life? Many times it is because they assume that they cannot learn or they might have disliked the way they were taught during their formal years of education, in the process developing a fear of learning.

Fortunately, we now know that we can learn from everything the mind perceives and at any age! **Dr. Benjamin Bloom**, who spent a lifetime studying excellence, has concluded that *"anyone can learn anything – the only difference is that some take more time than others."*

What will you learn today to make your life better tomorrow?

Action Steps

1. Though knowledge is powerful, it is not much use unless you ACT on it! In your journal, write down at the top of the page: "How can I increase my knowledge in my chosen topic?" It can relate to your work, it can also be about relationships, self-discovery, success, or anything else that you are currently thinking about and would like to know more about.
2. After you have written that question write 21 answers/action steps below. Choose 5 action steps from that list and act on them within a week. Then continue with the rest of the steps.

CHAPTER 51

YOU MAKE A DIFFERENCE!

"*Sharing makes you bigger than you are. The more you pour out, the more life will be able to pour in.*" – **Jim Rohn**

Did you ever think about making a difference in this world but felt you were not powerful enough to do that? I would like to share with you a wonderful story about sharing and making a difference that might change your mind:

A man was walking along a beach, reflecting on his life. He had always wanted to make a difference, but no matter what he tried, he wound up feeling as though he was spitting into the wind.

Suddenly, the man heard a loud "crunch," and looked down at his feet. Right where he was standing and as far as the eye could see in either direction, there were thousands upon thousands of tiny starfish washed up onto the shore by the ocean waves and tide.

The man continued walking thinking to himself about the apparent cruelty of the ocean. After all, those starfish hadn't done anything wrong! Yet before the day was done, they would be dead, washed up on the shore and left to die.

After a time, the man came across a woman standing at the ocean's edge, throwing starfish back into the sea. When he asked her what she was doing, she said she had always wanted to make a difference and had decided that today was a good day to start.

The man looked from her to the thousands upon thousands of starfish that lay dying along the coastline and said, "For every starfish you throw back into the ocean, three more wash up onto the shore! How can you possibly be making a difference?"

The woman looked thoughtful for a moment, then she picked up another starfish and threw it back into the sea.

"Made a difference to THAT one!" she said, with the most beautiful smile the man had ever seen.

Action Steps

1. To make a difference, one does not have to wait for some big moment, for when the time is right, for when there is more money to donate or more time to give. You have the opportunities and the power to make a difference every day of your life. Compliment someone, smile, give your undivided attention when someone speaks to you, let people know how much they mean to you, share this book with them. The list of small things that can make a big difference is endless...
2. Commit right now to add to someone's happiness today and every day UNCONDITIONALLY and don't forget to include YOURSELF on that list!

CHAPTER 52

CAN ONE PERSON CHANGE THE WORLD?

"*You are where you are and what you are because of what you believe yourself to be. Change your beliefs and you change your reality.*" – **Brian Tracy**

Do you believe one person can change the world? Do you believe it can be you?

In 1961 **Edward Lorenz**, a research meteorologist at the Massachusetts Institute of Technology who created a computer program designed to model the weather, has made an amazing discovery. As he was making the weather printout for the day, he decided to take a shortcut and typed the numbers in from the earlier printout midway through. An unexpected thing happened – his simulated new weather pattern had diverged dramatically from the previous printout!

Thinking his computer had malfunctioned, Mr. Lorenz examined the situation to discover that there was nothing wrong with the computer but with the numbers he plugged in. In the original program he had used six decimal places: .506127. In the second run he had rounded off the numbers to .506. He assumed that the difference – one part in a thousand – would have no real impact. He was wrong.

This slight change had made a HUGE difference. This tiny change in input had quickly created an overwhelmingly different output. The formal name for this phenomenon is "sensitive dependence on initial conditions." Its informal and more popular name is the *Butterfly Effect*. Simply stated, it means that the tiny changes brought about by a butterfly moving its wings in San Francisco have the power to transform the weather conditions in Shanghai!

Just think about it, if the tiny movements of a butterfly's wings can change the weather patterns across the world, how much change can YOU make by just one action? One thought? One wish or intention at a time?

What if you do it consistently?

Drawing on this respected scientific theory, I believe that you can accomplish miracles and amazing things with your life just by taking consistent focused actions in the direction of your dreams and goals!

Can One Person Change the World? | 119

> **Action Steps**
>
> Understand that everything you do and even think affects this world. HOW you will affect it, is up to you!

CHAPTER 53

IT IS NEVER TOO LATE

"*It is never too late to be what you might have been.*" – **George Elliot**, (1819–1880 English novelist)

Have you ever felt like it was too late to follow your dreams? Too late to discover and live the life of your purpose? If you have, than this story might inspire you:

> It was registration day at the university, and the young man was preparing to continue the adventure in learning that had been going on so long it seemed to have no beginning and no end. Lost in thought, his mind racing with possibilities for what lay ahead, he barely noticed the old man in front of him until he bumped straight into him.
>
> "I am sorry, professor," the young man said, embarrassed.
>
> "Oh, I'm not a professor," the old man replied. "I'm a new student, just like you."
>
> "But how old are you?" the young man said in shock.
>
> "I am 73," the old man said with a twinkle in his eye.
>
> "And what are you studying?" the young man continued.
>
> "Medicine – I've always wanted to be a doctor, and now…" The old man paused as if remembering something from a long time ago. "Now, I'm finally ready to follow my dreams!"
>
> The young man seemed quite shocked. "No disrespect sir, but to become a doctor will take at least 7 years. In 7 years, you'll be 80 years old! The old man put his hand on the young man's shoulder and looked him straight in the eyes.
>
> "God willing" the old man smiled, "I will be 80 years old whether I follow my dreams or not."

Action Steps

I always say to myself and to others that it is better to be truly happy and fulfilled for one hour than never. It is better to strive and work hard towards an inspiring goal than always wonder "what if..."

I know people who started to follow their dreams after they retired and became super successful in every way. I know people who fell madly in love at almost 70 years old, got married and now live blissfully happy lives…

It is NEVER to late. The only limitations you have are the limitations of your own mind and your belief system! Have the courage to go after your heart's desires and experience what real fulfillment and happiness is.

CONCLUSION
THE MOST IMPORTANT JOB YOU DO

"*Make the most of yourself, for that is all there is of you.*" – **Ralph Waldo Emerson**, (1803–1882 American author, poet and philosopher)

What is the most important job that you do? I believe that the most important job you do is the one that is unheard and unseen! The most important job you do happens WITHIN.

It is the journey to becoming the best you can be. It is becoming the kind of person who attracts all that you want in life. The most important job you do, is getting to know yourself – who YOU are, what YOU want to have, to do and to BE in this life.

You become the best you can be by taking your time to be with yourself, to understand your wants and needs, to understand and honor your uniqueness.

You do it by realizing that YOU are in control of your life and your future and by taking consistent actions to create that future – taking full responsibility rather than blaming circumstances.

Action Steps

1. Before you move on to the next page, before you close this book and immerse yourself into your day-to-day tasks, please take your calendar and schedule a date... with YOURSELF! It doesn't matter if you schedule a full day or just 20 minutes. As long as you know that this time is just for YOU – to do what you want, to think what you want, to just be. It is the time to honor yourself as someone important enough to be with.
2. Make an ongoing date, a time or a day you can look forward to.
3. Be patient, be good to yourself, and enjoy the journey!

REFERENCES AND RECOMMENDED READING

These are some of the books and programs that influenced and changed my life. Many of the books and authors below are also mentioned and quoted throughout The One Minute Coach™. They are listed in alphabetical order.

7 Habits of Highly Effective People, The by Stephen Covey
11th Element, The by Robert Scheinfeld
100 Absolutely Unbreakable Laws of Business Success, The by Brian Tracy
Abundance for Life: Trance Breaking, Wealth Making by Paul R. Scheele
Accelerated Learning (audio program) by Colin Rose & Brian Tracy
Alchemist, The by Paulo Coelho
Awaken the Giant Within by Anthony Robbins
Celestine Prophesy, The by James Redfield
Change Your Life in 7 Days by Paul McKenna
Chicken Soup for the Soul by M. Victor Hansen & Jack Canfield
Conversations with God by Neale Donald Walsch
Einstein Factor, The by Win Wenger & Richard Poe
Empty Chair, The: Finding Hope and Joy by Rabbi Nachman of Breslov
Focal Point by Brian Tracy
Greatest Salesman in the World, The by Og Mandino
How to Win Friends & Influence People by Dale Carnegie
Leadership Challenge, The by J. M Kouzes & B.Z Posner
Leadership Wisdom from the Monk who Sold His Ferrari by Robin Sharma
Life 101 by Peter McWilliams
Little Book of Coaching, The by Ken Blanchard and Don Shula
Many Lives, Many Masters by Brian L. Weiss
Master Thinker Program (workshop) by Dr. Bill Gould.
One Minute Manager, The by Kenneth H. Blanchard and Spencer Johnson

One Minute Millionaire, The by Victor Hansen & Robert G. Allen
Personal Power II: The Driving Force (audio program) by Anthony Robbins
Power of Purpose, The by Richard Leider
Profit, The by Khalil Gibran
Psychology of Achievement, The (audio program) by Brian Tracy
Rich Dad Poor Dad by Robert Kiyosaki
Seat of the Soul, The by Gary Zukav
Secrets about Men Every Woman Should Know by Barbara de Angelis
Sedona Method, The by Hale Dwoskin
Think and Grow Rich by Napoleon Hill
Who Moved My Cheese by Spencer Johnson and Kenneth H. Blanchard

Please visit www.mashamalka.com to read a summary for each of these books and/or to purchase them.

Thank you!

ABOUT THE ARTIST

Anna Polonsky is a Florida based multimedia artist who explores the realm of imagination in both digital and traditional mediums. Her skills range from graphic design and vector illustrations to traditional paintings and sculptures. As a passionate visual content creator, she has taken on challenging projects and has worked with clients from all around the world, across a wide array of industries such as architecture, entertainment, manufacturing and more. Anna is driven by the vision of creating works of art that will encourage artists and non-artists alike to open their minds toward the realm of imagination and the power of thought.

Working with Masha on this incredibly empowering publication has truly made a positive impact on Anna's art, helping her to create every image in this book into something that will inspire others.

To contact Anna please write to: polonskyart@gmail.com or visit www.annapolonskyart.com

ABOUT THE AUTHOR

Masha Malka is a Russian/American who spends her time living between Sunny Isles, Florida and Marbella, Spain. She is a best-selling author and founder of The One Minute Coach™ educational system. She has worked as an executive coach for over 15 years; built a successful import and distribution company; taught Business Leadership at MUIC; won Ballroom competitions; got her Master's Degree in Higher Education while raising three children. Masha also has training certificates in Accelerated Learning Techniques and Transformational Thinking, Graduate Certificate in Teaching and Training Online and a diploma in Clinical Hypnotherapy. She is an author of *Discover Your Inborn Genius e-book*; a contributing author to the *Chicken Soup for the Soul: Power Moms*; the *Power of Persistence* book; *Achieve Your Ultimate Success* DVD, and much more.

The experiences of overcoming the struggles of being a refugee at 17 years old, dealing with a very difficult break-up of a 20-year marriage, living in seven countries, coaching hundreds of people around the world and constantly learning, researching and applying her knowledge, have all made this book possible.

To learn more about Masha Malka and her programs, please visit www.mashamalka.com

THANK YOU

This was just the start of your journey to emotional mastery...

| **mashamalka.com/gifts** |

The One Minute Coach™ system is much more than *one book* can hold.

It's the answer to frustration, challenges, or fears that might be holding you back from the life you truly want to create.

You *don't* have to do this alone!

Step 1: Visit **mashamalka.com/gifts** – where you'll discover more about the power of The One Minute Coaching. I'll personally guide you through exactly how to begin using the exercises in the book, give you more tips on how to stay focused one minute at a time, and share more about how emotional mastery can transform your life and your results.

Step 2: After claiming your free gifts, you'll register to become part of The One Minute Coach Community. The community includes fresh exercises, videos, and opportunities for you to connect with others on the same journey as you.

Again – just visit **mashamalka.com/gifts** to get your gifts now.

As you've seen from the years of research and work that have gone into creating The One Minute Coach, I'm completely committed to helping you create results in any area of your life.

This book is just designed to be your starting point. There are many additional ways to get support and stay focused on your journey of transformation.

I look forward to supporting you in all areas of your destiny!

Visit **mashamalka.com/gifts** now for much more.

With love and gratitude,

Masha Malka

www.ingramcontent.com/pod-product-compliance
Lightning Source LLC
Chambersburg PA
CBHW070054120526
44588CB00033B/1435